lollyology

Derek Motion

First Published 2012 by Derek Motion

Derek is a supporter of Garamond

Cataloguing-in-Publication Data

National Library of Australia

Motion, Derek.

lollyology.

ISBN 978-1-105-76228-4

I. Title

A821.4

Acknowledgements

I am grateful for the support given to me by the editors of the following journals, where poems from this book have first appeared or been republished:

> *The Age, Blue Dog, The Best Australian Poems 2009, The Best Australian Poems 2010, Cordite Poetry Review, Ecopoetics, fourW, Going Down Swinging, [Growling Softly]* (USA), *HEAT, Overland, Page Seventeen, Prosopisia* (India), *Southerly, Some Sonnets, The Sun Herald,* and *Verity La.*

Some of these poems have also first been made public in draft form on my blog: *typingspace.com.au/blog*

This manuscript was completed with the assistance of an emerging writers grant from the Australian Society of Authors / The Australia Council for the Arts.

Contents

x

y

z

X

one

drinking seven beers standing up

but then it's yesterday's kids' party

(light plays over a cake it's an eight it's

shaped like a race-track (the standing

the thing to remember & also there are

people looking like characters from macbeth

they are in various stages of decay (makes you

smile (there is probably haiku sentiment

on the wind outside (where cricket

was discarded (a while back

the bat stands there

gumi

i'd take a bag of flour in the face
for you i'd snag my heart on the
bottom the river blithe as freddo
frog scraping the surface in a mist
of public liabilities i'll scrawl your
initials on a crusted pylon this is the
way i show affection &/or my trophyish
status in a land of freaks i'm so cool
i'm miles up a tree above you all &
i'm several times drunk launching
myself off the rocks i'm all things to
you a snag & some hyphenated cattle
so love me in aerosol terms don't
even laugh if i tether my dog to
this plastic afternoon machine

hush

often chloroform undertones in the banana-scented
musics of the street some more cigarettes splice
your fingers & proffer themselves   like
the people of boston might trevor laid the ground-
work for the night's running joke   ice ruining
a blissful feeling that simply could have been
unlike frayed paralysis never the mcdonalds logic
of contemporary insurance micko thinks you
can protect your family from a sit-com death or
waxen misunderstandings turned bad he's not
cultured but speaks of it sanely   in a swell
psych-experiment you're a younger friend an
initiate verging on the acolytic   if you'll underline
my content riddled thought with heath ledger-esque
delivery once   more the moon might spit chunks
the candelabra might appear   outdated we're
destined to repeat our boredoms the result statistically
significant if you like (from behind those glasses

ode

does this celebrate your essence now, your
lofted heights? this call to all shaky one-
times & moments / chunks of narrative
erased by   necessity & lost dances,
cheeks, blank-stares et cetera

does this googling place your spirit now as you
work through a virtual tsunami of companies,
shuffling *i don't knows* into a middle-age, one
readers / clients picture inaccurately

does your husband offer his feelings at ceremonies
or just bark at turning trucks? are you mean to him
like me? is money a likely return?

i've ranged over the other poems
inked things celebrating your aspects

& this is just so you know

regional

my bed was my castle
then i grew into a boyfriend

now thought can't catch me

long saturday mornings there are
other things to do

blank distance the daft overlay
for all the weigh-bridge towns
we didn't grow up in, but plain dissected

quainter in hindsight though symbolic,
visualise one hypercolour agri-checkerboard,
canola the teen & adult yardstick

your heavy metal siblings forming a purpose
of social scenery: hard liquor off-limits until
the appointed hour: barricades stormed
for the steaming twilight anecdotal

mosquitoes swoop the sheets
interrupting aural voyeurism & so what

now i am the centre of any *real* conversation

grown into one half of this landed couple:
the hotel / motel of never-ending scope

a matter of seconds

the girl across the oval she is much
younger as the girl at your school she
is much older as the mother of however
many that still dresses in black & orders
several hair foils for a hundred bucks a
last gasp gesture to outlandishness now
she takes a moment a matter of seconds
to swap empty words with a guy & he
is quite content as this nobody until he
moves his cap & reveals himself
another someone from that school a
person you never spoke to but his image
sticks smashed into your synapses like
the snail you felt collapse under your
toes once your awkward self realising
the necessity of moving some rubbish
bins in the rain & whimsically going
at it barefoot the pure sensation of things
not often what it could be like two
people exerting a vague connective
influence like a duo of extras in a
pirate movie you know they've done
something else you probably liked it
but now they are pirates, strangers

i'd interview you too

when late shows come on tv & hours conspire to tiredness.
isn't this a 'really' issue: the curlews rife in your works like
local hills, fading to a crisp purple; a puppet always the first
thought, or erotic conceits, some just failures. everyone
an openly non-believing head of state. phwt phwt. aaar.

we flow through a choice of spectacles & wags care to write
of the 'really really' world & i want to live there but i didn't.
i'll auspice you in creamy broadsheets: words are not counted
despite craving it, shivers felt under the oft close dogma.

you're a man of great feminine capacity – your style
is the time of moments passing. most of the ozone
layers are just out there doing their jobs. like bell-curves
we're sad in the morning then complacent later then sad again.
flossing mint lolly teeth is now work for the best boy, a shadow.

becoming a tourist attraction

it's more work than it seems like loading shoot-em-
ups from cassette or sweltering waiting for a girl
with crimped hair the knock on your window interrupting
imaginary piano a duet with elton john   3am
the pine roofing glows or maybe the ebony & browning ivory
imprints are cryptic codes in your mind / hope for a password
or a cheat (programmers abnormally fixate on douglas
adams) all the while mum & dad's tv is the apocalypse too
or at least death coming from miles away
down the hallway   the rabbit ears just a blur
what at first was a good idea a holiday sort of deviation
with RACQ caravanning stickers with fifty cents to spend
on redskins & spearmint sticks & milk bottles it
now lacks the comfort of those past ideas   there's always
better & more expensive joysticks to fondle there's always
a kid called chris around the corner with his own basketball hoop
(careful   don't say there's nothing to do)
before you know it several holistic craft shops will open
but they're all selling collectible magic cards & tobacco
& anyway   your dad is still saying goodbye   going to live
in a small box the tv now mounted on the wall
only some kind of black struts keeping   it
from hitting the floor

vocabulary

olivia ramshackle amidst a blitz
of acacia spume, swears to remain
exterior to 'i love you', forgets her purse.
a blatant mine of perfumed gadgetry &
archaic post-it text though. we admire her:
her windswept pose looking like lost lipstick
on early film stock, all the gaudy reds & greens,
a shock of skittles colour, hair slightly over-long
for this stage of modernity. i was away
from the set-piece filling in a time-sheet
with aplomb registering the dots / dashes /
irate minutes of labour. but yet. but still.
wild thistle & hairy panic circling
the edges of the frame, masking olivia
& her age; peals of bird issuing a tonal
cusp, a things-must-change like
the weather ultimatum, borderline
romance. her severe hemline gazing
at me through space, battling a
fractal geometry of twig &
brush, affording itself status
as image. we work on
mustering a sufficient
& valid ode.

brendan went to NIDA

in this brief epoch we ache of sitting down kerplunk.
suffer occasional blindness – earphones crumbling –
reserve carparks amidst alienating & thought-of flowers
sadly, just because. some forms perforated,
shipwrecks gone awol. whomever my stuffed-
animals would reify in their boredom wakes
in the cupboard. alarm-clock of synesthestic intent,
mulled ideation under roof-beams (well
darker in any *what* of earth spin) suggests
beaches, people checking eggs, 'the', bindies.

'for' inside & roasting a mallowed question
life is foxy. just one pash in the blanket-
graveyard of yet-to-do, of pastel insinuations.
if miracles eventuate maybe begin to sketch
your dog in the nude glancing away. our worst
opposites got less different in every ashbery poem,
certainly long recipes gyrate. i'm gone shouting
intractable slogans to wagons on the country road &
technology has a demeanour. go fuck yourself.

ballet lies

host on the host with every addition a
round earth becky from an angle is amplified
over the gate days device cooling off the bmx
the wonders of the boys never do stop to slide
from a bag of unlimited power jubes in pocket
i fold down in order to take one currency from
five centuries tenacious thought of cylindrical
teeth glare as the news crews think next to '&'
& a grinding of pvc over elastic; the sticks
presuppose you only i bracelet bill-posters in my
mind, however, in order to develop itself here in all
the green sparkling, a girl has need of things:

a cherry ripe of speed distortion thus beautiful like
wrists on a sweater, fleecy-you behind a watch of
years & more successive; tasks to be something
some thing a mirror-sphere concentrates in on
home-made silk roomy people insignificant in it
the external discord a game of soccer the group
nobody passed behind till the angry drunk then
or something approximately & becky:

friends or wants to be based near me a moment,
with acute perfect afternoon is for warmth
of proximity with a new vigilance that champion
is unexpected, you can always say the things
it crushes a nothing & some girls who do not know
my secrets: how much the more i am regulated
in order to transform myself moreover how
loquacious i will seem not to point out the parka-
blue i will develop myself occasionally from the lack

things

water to watermark gap, canvas of the tree,
about two feet. toaster's increased browning
capacity, a result of past usage. so clever.
i have frittered away my time.

a starling baby plop from its nest. &
the hidden wine casks. do you
utilise theory? we should go for a walk.

it has certainly warmed up, hasn't it.
that's the old butcher's shop front.
over there, you could buy drugs.

do you have eftpos? thanks for
picking me up. i've been on track,
lately. i feel older.

observational #8 (commodore V8)

the blokes battle torsion leaning said ute like a mechanical-bull
    (lucrative pro-racing careers dependant on style)
finite police-cars embedded in a stray hill, here & there. okay,

descript objects are thinning out: i glanced at my neighbour
through his shower window – must have been around the 15th –
& he considered his penis carefully. nothing perverse in it, or
me. i suspect old buildings of motives too, grand of scope &
utilised in hindsight, caught by instances of small-town:
libraries, churches, mechanics' institutes. as if by chance.

people flounder about their living in the vaults & vestries,
sacrosanct while i slam the car-boot with a final emphasis.
it knows i will be back: a look about the headlights. onward &
then roads continue to spider off other roads justly closed, eroded
& signed as such. all visible moments inviting like reading murder
details in the papers. i hope to make more sense of things –
the objects, the projects, the overarching directions – this month.

tupperware

we saw derek making a cup of tea: ½ turn, ¼ turn,
angel falls of sugar & the water blinked away.
a chipped china absence & you'd guess the cup
messed with the wrong glass (nightclub of
suds). derek effected this beverage to then sit
on a freezer & compost the adjunct images.
caffeine still leeching as if the pondering
was not just inopportune but obscene. 10
mins at the traffic lights. standing at the
wrong counter. the hamburgular's in-store
appearance. derek seemed assured, such
instances fell ably to hand & often, perhaps a
quantifiable result of the heuristic honours thesis.
he massaged his right shoulder strained from
the irate nothingness repeated for too long.
he removed the teabag quashing a remainder
between thumb & forefinger. we eyed derek,
the arbiter of all final actions; mid-court rallies.
derek leaves off more tensile pursuits to drink tea.
he imagines it will jostle the senses & afford direction,
or so we suppose, observing because life is boring.

own chef opinion

blue an arc of bristling cloud unwinds
into the eyes dejected & elated in waves,
all such steaming repetition boggles sheer
stainless steel: everywhere & nowhere & in-
between (so, i was sitting there writing
about these huge clouds this steam that
shouldn't be there, & i was thinking, wow,
this is major, & you just know *something*
is going on (unexpected the flaming ad-break
segue reinforces my slavish behaviour, so,
i scratched your silver macbook casing
anticipating thoughts of the past,
daguerreotype-like, wordless & pristine
(i was sitting scratching, lip crust of caramello
residue, when suddenly, finally, it clicked:
something where something happens!
not the typical aha to invoke emotion,
flaccid attendant randomness no (this is the
judging of food: i was standing this time,
being judged & i was thinking, this is it you know,
real judgement, but somehow simultaneously
at least it's real & there, no flimsy fiction of
appellative talent, just the pert gust of wet &
noisome air unbroken before the moment had
passed (i was suspecting as much (so, i was)

june was first

june was the first girl rodney ever
talked to about his feelings he remembers
the spore of an unknown plant drifting past
her lobes an unknown amount of distance
through a window the consolation he is offered
for wasted romance is a glimpse of an idea he
conceived back around june or july it involved
a mode of transport & the patenting of a small
tweak that would make it slightly more efficient
he realises the improvement has since been made &
perhaps was even back then when june kissed him &
let his hands rove but only certain parts of her body
it's those parts that would be nice for rodney
to know again that would be a real consolation
one befitting gloomy afternoons where he
gets not much done but organises an electrician
to install something in his house then decides
the teabags deserve a more prominent
position in the cupboard: it's how his life
is going at the moment

y

feelings

brianna pushed steve no-one could've expected that
the taxi-rank still flourishing sometime near the early
hours removed him from place like superfluous words
edited falling into victoria park he yells an effort lost to
engines & road & sirens once reading levertov her use of
plucking i read as *fucking* steve was dyslexic too
never bothered us though his removal by brianna the
bit of blood & his sure clique ejection might've cured him only
ghosts there though listening to some obscure lines he takes away
fragments of syntax muttered at a desk-sergeant & the night

lyric to signal my knowing

scooter my experimental garden-path sugared mint leaves
see the light of day mauled by every species of roach maybe
eight so numerous a tally exhumed at the door death but lacking of
gleam go forth rubbered grips crack anyway paddle-pop stick limbs
fuse to the road your best friend of convenience bristles
a jolt forces red hair up he's telling the big-side boys to fuck off
crazed not much else in this remake just a skivvy & afl teachers
doing a nipple-dance let us retreat & mime / cough romantic excuses
out excavate like a bleached ball & reanimate the kid docile to
bury headless barbie mid-autumn vacuous a year to schedule intensity
back a season or two tune instrumental arrays into 440hz
fights are nightly & nicely & bright in paved mania assume some blitz
to coordinate the yoyo hula the moon as it signals 'hearth'
or the slated tussle of unforgettable chow mien

life in the miniature steam-train village

some of us do stay here   i have a room under
the miniature tunnel the door is a drain-cover

a secret i open only when the tourists have gone

some of the overalled men have wives & they are civil
in fact they smile more than us 'residents'

they often drink from thermoses

they tinker with the engines they collect tickets
    but then they go home

some wives are dead & so we move in here

there are various parts of the community vacant
one hair-pin down near the petunia bed & estuary in particular

that corner has a bad feel to it: the site of a derailing
    back in the 70s it's our equivalent of cheap-real-estate

train-enthusiasts are superstitious   with good reason
on purple nights when we all gather to drink beer & spin
monologues around the tiny turnpike   then perfectly scaled spirits walk

the village comes alive with their spectral whispers

some seem to catch in my beard   a mixture of human cries

(the justly dead span generations   the boy gurgling in the water not
yet talking   to the heart-attack veterans out for one last reminisce)   but

also the fairies we created ourselves giggle
the dwarves cease their mining & gather to connive

there is a swarthy & strange life in this place it
is pungent at times   i run the trains by day

      by night   under the tunnel   i write

inadequate stovetop

i lap up macadamia fuzz in a middle aged stroll of the 'nature'. espying a roof rack
means change the world instead, or try on sunglasses ingested by a seven-eleven,
or read emily bitto's poem & feign a partner's formal awareness. hum,
like mythic solitary couples sparse atop 'fauna'.

anyway you're bubbly. & less lcd in spirit becalmed in those spurts. as spun
wool wet suited & vast they find nothing in my head no feeling no tartan
gift wrapping (though such curling patterns fuck around in dreams, wax
semi-porous opinion). a vaseline moment & a 'perfect' sticker
affixed to my clothes. all hot, lovely, or so
my jaw speculates.

over to gorgon youths barraging the heads. girls venture further
& nakeder to peruse the bluster. a blyton shark net hole looses seals
& one lone stingray, a smoker, a maverick snorkeler, is fictional.

living bends my spine in & out of that stuporific posture, a useful
talking point. we meandered into the joust talk like sand djinns,
far-limited by day… now bleached into a pathetic fade of umber,

as a footnote of who will hold the mantle? years ahead in what
might be glum future, else bank queues   he stops to borrow
all your stuff – hat flippers coat wallet – with me a carefree grin
they can only breed, then locks under the spume with definite
activity / mindful of things i disappear. awful profundity in the wind.

the huntsman's legs extended with a passing thunderhead.

our party has become a spider, grappling to predict equal change in feeding ritual.
lime infused tea vomits a vapour of muzak to our traversal of polarization of
digital means – to move / to get static / to tape 'obstinate' & bend it through a
low-pass filter, to imagine only the background level subject matter ever:

irony as a head slap / falling from a car after. you're a tool.

you could enter into more details. then, there. an academic reference
to richard gere's rehearsed lines seems slight, in hindsight.
i discovered the tomes on everything (passing forest, firetrails named
after his grave, packets of 'big things' & the website to back you up)
but everyone else is incapable of feeling the same awkward.

in houses bereft of for sale signs, boats parked round the side, we'll straggle.
down a murderous side-path not obvious to light. here's a picnic bench,
a council bin. streaks of wind across some dwindle of bay.
i'm seeking resonance. rub cream into the stings,
& elsewhere, all quarters pleasurable.

the bream flounders under his stern gaze. no worries
blown across, telegraphed as a sentence, whole.

pelmet manufacturer

my life was a role-playing game
without beards or tankards
we took a swift kite out in the blur
making proof of my mood fixed
things in this postcard-of-ale tuesday
sugared strawberries woolworths madness
broadband bills arresting from the gutter-
vantage mocking the ruffian the nearby
'go awol with me mate no problems' instinct
but no if you would like to listen to the choir
press 1 when your mind is a smacked gob
it's always the shuffle of pension day &
are you a homeowner (what type of car
do you drive how do you cope etc)
have you liked anything recently
or can we mend this i don't see how
my life is a choking hazard

forest hill

tall / pondering a nose scratch

the still-dark hall lies await starboard
a wan incitement to futures of regression
(we'll sift a plastery dust of cobain chords alone,
re-vaunt his prattle perhaps)

everything was about the lack of a large hat

now flattened grass directs me.
past the lit blobs of wall post-midnight, a vain reconnaissance
of avenues hamletting the refitted butchers – teens secure
abreast stunted cherry limbs – where we all question
a growing emphasis internally: 'when you grow up?'

you shouldn't trust in lines. insist on the classic
frippery of a stackhatted boy, or a soundbyte boy
still high on wit & abc arabesques,
not yet worried

as oft-gazed-at windows reflect traffic-
light over moon & defy your romance distillation

chunks of smaller faddish moments were piled up in
a mountain of sexual cliché – milestones on the record
as dumb gesture, a word or two hyperbolic even amidst years
        (a backseat to queensland / a trilogy of dragon questing)

& it's obvious. i'm unearthing the school's time-capsule, secretly, after nightfall. the balaclava didn't even involve a choice. i edit scathingly. i mock the other raaf kids' dreams. i make a claggy pulp out of their failed foundation cursive. at the bubblers i consider sobbing for their facebook realities, but instead do this. i re-inter. i prance through the half-formed stimulus buildings like non-threatening catacombs. biggles-like.

funny, your shadow apes a testing rodent in such light

i like to worry the mosquitos away with my own hand
a caress or a simple command to the dog this too says *living* like
no other minor-farce courting experience courting a teasing *closetoyouness*
it smells of ruin sometimes (& if you're saying that to hurt me i like it,
seriously, do it again, red rover cross over)

again   uncool with every collection of coin & stamp
my growing freedom was grounded
by bic-pen blow-darts

choices were plotted as 'outliers' to expose for others
all the reasons you would eye people, then look down,

for always now, friends are stuck in period dress with
appropriate fringes, like elle macpherson appliquéd to some
important magazine tooth weft   knowingly touched to

for always now, friends are emceed to a hush.
quadrangle slights are all there is. just lie there
divorced & unknown. like the interlocutors
filmed in 80s hues you are or were.

i am awful disconnected   huddled in a first-person
white – aching for a goldfield souvenir, reawakening on the bus

& no one lives anywhere anymore. i spent the morning searching the knolls of geography. there is nothing, not a seed-scrape of the crazed backyard vegetable purveyor, no memorial to the place we found a telephone number on post-it. i dialled randomly at the phonebox anyway. i said 'who lives here?' in order to begin the mystery again. the next clue is inside the hollow log, hidden by the patterson's curse at the centre of the dirt-track, now developed into housing.

we attend the adult meditation on craft,
assembly, & routine,
& plan reunions

underneath
there's a scratch of reel-to-reel flicker

a casual netball skirt whistle

Invasion

1

we're phantasmagoric & over fed square (post eco parking post
an ill-thought dumplings ploy & the odour of spilling soy)
even to interiors breasting a ship's plushie aspect, mounting
layer upon player so as to ply a drink with waving departure

one small glass. the slops still a veritable ambrosia
toes rocking above head level
still, you sleep.

a big steam breakfast the instinct to knowingness,
else timelessness, it's all appropriate. only one image lures
you past alternate fog (westerly):

a ponderous sea dragon growing without effort.
(mottled pink & supreme in having time-to-think)
it's so unlike us all, so worthy of permanent capture,
meditative study.

with such fitful poise I'd grace
any maccas carpark.

2

another fist of views means, erratically, you're au fait
with the ice danger – 'views' lack speed indicators,
all twists & turns simply set to parallel all things,
all the time. I think in bytes. you know, inspired, irate,

worried, inspired… we crest a township to find a cottage &
drag the strip. come on! observe this stodgy boat ramp &
kids ranting lysergic fishing lore. (oh, later: the ethics
of fish & chips vs. local ale) slabs of information
dot each pier even through our coverage blackspot.

electric-blanket-land stirs a temporary love affair,
& this adam sandler movie set amidst 'coastlines',
only half dismaying in its todayness, its watchability.

get into the straightest of passages: tercentennial ferry
to a site of industry / brunch over the car & re-pack the run off.
rod slam & scooter blitz into the back of a good showering –
ample views of life, hills, unscrupulous poetry to an audience
fighting back dadaist southern life (hence the flagrant repetition)
shipping news vernacular like, starboard over, & over, this
simply matters or doesn't.

one comment is the renaissance (check out my website!)
but stake a base removal from the bar as effective, for kicks,
then beat the life out of a skate park. scour an Indian restaurant
for cricket memorabilia, or even candy coated fennel seeds &
the taste of your bed's silly refusal of feet… a noisome cat
is far better than the ache, parsed as perpetual.

our chocolate coated lives: words exist for this process:
to ooze through when hot, our skins a foil, all presupposed
to hide a bitter patent of the colour purple (as it seems
in purple dreams). the blonde girl assures us / me / of her addictions.
no less confident with such things impending. but cut from her
to botany / musical play equipment / the ways we name
living things / science / the arousal of suspicion…

I photograph Violet to isolate her as a growing thing,

txt it via pizza hut one mind on the powerful & loud
faux-teens. it's a delight & absolute. a proud gourmet
variety of people kept in the cellar. there is always tv.

Hobart began with a block, two couples kissing,
frozen out the window by my glance. this place
of love, public beauty. suppose this.

3

memories of killing can only be stomached with food.
food again destroying your silly faith in Capitalism
(you plan to order the t-shirt) everything feeling
less systematic than it should. former towns are
pretty & uniformly un-guarded

suffice to say I'd play up the history of a place – as if
active agency were involved – but only if the mental gap
were appropriate. (like a 19th century pick axe to the skull
it's barbaric but expected, though always worth putting your
hand up for, a tactile reworking of 'stickiness', an intellectual
act of baravado). Bryant taking to tourists so recently though,
this blooms disquiet. the recent ghosts are marginalized.
predictable. a tour through the genuine reality of the
solitary wing & I wish the group away, I feel,
quickly, what a sense of real feeling could be
(how you hate the others)

4

not bored with the scent of huon pine. repacking

in ever looser segments, clothes like the blots
of wildlife preserved out there. we spot-fish illegally,
again, parade past the eco-toilet, again,
just as eyer-boggled as starfish on the bay.
like at the caravan park convenience store –
nobody wants what you have… with that
we rejoice. spiffy little carved train carriages,
all soon noted, even in the hazy laugh-pod of first class.
endless booze clarifies the mist.

I'm carrying a sassafras twig all day, by touch
mentally rechecking the memories, two by two,
placing the odour as a pivotal future crutch.

remembrance of scents past.

this sprung beach at nightfall, defies watering down.
we are shadows glazed in gold-pink, captured
by the correct aperture, & we are at times
worth the danger.

rainforest blues / countless photo ops.

you'd pan for gold perpetually, given the time.
i give you mine
& wind the bus home
all things a question of credit.

5

the hedge maze is the permission we all need
to run to flail (kids make friends / I don't)

it casts into relief the world I wanted
to love (should have been a product of rigour)
it doesn't follow, but alcoholism is studiously observed.
I'll observe anything involving a boat. stumbling
past dubious deeds & the desire to meditate,
the lack of such follow through.

all you do is have the ability to know this.
service with a beep. armrest reading light.
the blackened essence of travel.
me pitching it at you.

design brief.pdf

the hard drive a still hum, a natural pilot light
to goad essentialism, wind bringing things out
into the rampant today of an open room.   'mojo'
skulks away misunderstood. a curtly folded media-release
flutter is your orchestra rustle. i'm lacking a train route
& just filling out the questionnaire / assured /
taking on the stakeholder persona, singing the department
store chorus above our heads: this won't be quoted correctly.
but laundry moments like they were before – the room humid
with cooking cotton, air a fractured cold out any such window.
even finding stashed cigarettes & bristling at the illogic,
how it becomes us.   summer dresses in winter;
the first thing in the cupboard.

a zombie stare of near to distant past mottles my voice,
irate voice of future negotiations. i can't decide. people
studied your poster & sticky tape while you hid deaf
against lighting structure, the public sculpture,
publicly keen as waxed apples on the table.
charging $5 for audience development
    (invoice me).

she thought the spaces suggested only limited things (meaning you were wrong that time). et cetera & for example, the better arrangement brings forth the more user-friendly interface, the more effective transmission of data, & absence won't imply infinite optioning. there is only to be the first assumption / the binary concession of inaction. you'd better prepare for scenarios that are delimited by a false a & b. else i'll sick my dog on you.

& so & so forth.
cluster bomb in the wendys.
the pink t-shirt loop.

you remember x talking about the system of
the longer tract (the apparent necessity) you
remember yourself repeating it (the uncertain
truism) & you remember y grasping it
with not too much enthusiasm. you you
you. how silly it all seems, lines from special-k
commercials in the 80's making a mockery
of your chaos-theory, the snickers wrapper
walking off to mate with a tolkien book.

the path to that lecture hall looks like touching a little puppy.
let it lick real madly & cutely at you. i can hear the
    protective way things wrap you up.

fate of the species

poets x, y, & z at different times. we talk of stray things –
x mentions Hawkesbury Country more than once, as if you can't
walk through it, not without feeling an owner's 'presence'.

y & i imagine who would win in kickboxing bouts,
the tough-looking poets or the wise?   (no rule emerges)

& z introduces someone, then pauses, stares at an adjacent wall,
quite forgetting the norms. an iconoclast. i don't know what to say:

anonymity is grand but still i love to fix a sly certain stretch of days
(ala Schuyler). though the days are not consecutive, three is a fine number.
i'll be in the present, feigning indifference towards a terrible driver.

my poor faculty to retort drifts out the car window,
my face noting a lack of sun, keys jangling morosely. that's cool.

then you'll be studying images of marine-life on a laptop, outdoors,
doing whatever 'thing' is in question by proxy. still in the present.

(you are you)

catching a titanic haul to feed the family is the fallacious banter, & yet
there is nothing like the peace before this evolutionary gambit

(modernly named children shoulder rods & pro-scooters their faces dripping with
saccharine & hate of things *other* they'll nod curtly in the
        curt distance

(as if the history of nods & that canon where nothing))

finally the glaze-over as colour grips a substation *there,* &

we gaze longingly at one sun plus one cloud plus the way
'dazzling' sort of dances along a gravel curve fronting some water,

all in keeping with the time: all so particular to *there*,
    the blanket antithesis of *here*. the real man vs beast action.

it's where you might almost see the ghost of St. Augustine
ambling along the banks… except i've only got a Bega vista to use,

or some comet-skies of Narooma, or the leaf-green Tilba trap.
(secretly poet x & i do battle for 'Riverina Country'
    where Cod would eye you if they could)

we were driving the incomplete road to Albury anyway when
y commented on the specificity of ghosts – it's an unremarkable stretch.
    petrol-stations seizing up & places bypassed. you wouldn't understand.

sure, your friends *will* get personal (despite studying rhetoric):
the speculative literature of personal revelation being just so intoxicating,

in that 'there is hope after all' way. it's not only substations though,
go-cart attendants call out names & the 'curt' kids navigate erratic ramps:

just as stop-start as the conversational play of z: & with that:
your past life with fish, else the c-grade tennis trophy, it's all in a photograph
& a message on the back appears to be scrawled, in a scrawled hand

'jim & frank 89', else a polaroid x, y, & z… it doesn't matter.
like real men coaxing valid responses from landmark landrovers,

petrol fumes & bird-sounds take you back to memorised land,
the exact numbers so spatially ill-determined, moral as August.

i'm nothing like the other men & that keeps the plovers well away.

when you mention 'property' (in a poem) three crows wail a symbolic rave:

it's you expressing a note of doubt (x a smudge off in the distance) &
the hamlet we aspire to a collection of insulated evils (men escape to 'weekender').

for now i'll reflect the lot in the slower breath after toil: a tractor balanced briefly
between long sky & uncertain rows of growth: ordered or otherwise nothing much is

indicative:

it's not your problem but here you'll feature large: like the birds you turned 'painstaking'
into a verb for, they loom in the adventures of x, y, z, as located by me
    in a series of landscapes we plain zip through.

tracing-paper

i love moving a rusted sleep-pattern
between the thighs of your exhaust

a drifting mobile of unflattering hemlines
ambles, spindrift as the inched string

& frost expands the world when invited

we can't continue to meet
like this lilac book-spine under finger

moon-tinted glass a romance of the apparent
& reflections come & go from curvatures

let's waste an immanent graphic spool, or seconds

apart in some theorised fixative
i suspect joggers hunt for love-letters

counting dwindles of dragon smoke every duped morning,
lives cast artfully between two minor dots of hill

stretched like headless mannequins on a map

the cut of clothing around the breast &
a swiftness in your hair colour well

sexy bleakness gets abrupt (para-everything),
the locale a place-of-many silences, else flaring loves

fold-out autumn

historical periods (the rustic modes of transport & dress)
appeal to the 'motion pictures'. things are cyclical. you
know: one canberra afternoon it's france circa eighteenth
century, done with an edgy eighties colour saturation.

like first-blush, opened fantales, or your everyday dinner-guests who
reach their fifties, then seize power in a semi-legitimate democracy.
visuals too often a distraction from life or that girl: always younger,
or steadfastly naked, valuing the way she evolves within your eyes.
a returned gaze. nice – apostrophes stretching futureward
became possessive. people in major-centres were your friends too,
though they now wear current trends on the body & ooze blasé.

(i'm studying leather-jacket-wearing: the pure numbers, proportions)

everything is nice, sure: a median-strip cutting the greater
population into odd halves. but you have to imagine stool-pigeons
haven't cut all the data yet, or made the recommendations we'll follow.
public-servants were using phraseology like 'integrated services'
(once) & 'structured redistribution' only first they would define their
make-up. (woden: we're back!) after all, the arts minister did
front the press-conference near a disabled toilet. the delegates
leaking 'tired' while pushing 'spritely'.

if you'd like to look straight down my mouth, estimate
an honest diameter, a coarse measure of aptitude, do so.
rip the awkward lace from a chairwoman's business-suit
in the process. it all goes together. think of inanimate objects –
court them. i feel proud of myself shopping. goods unfold
in an array of gold & red; we feel things doubly.

speculative #1

you calibrate & catch fleetingly the moment of a baby calming
with the chill of backyard half-sky. it contrasts well, takes you

to ken bolton's inane sunlit coffees & thoughts. & you think,
well, why not store & remember this, for later endeavours? if

only the manoeuvres were so easy, like using cliché the word
within a poem, it's a cliché & not much of one. you gather

the empty cat-tins & purposefully wind down. then eat some
biscuits. atoms & secret signals unite to push the elements,

nudging you toward a stray thing. cigarette ash collects
in a certain corner of the patio. the dog avoids it, lists

from his own illness, positioned starboard. you are a
scavenger of your own experiences. you teach the baby

art in your spare time. & together you fight post-apocalyptic
evil, or will. you proffer an opinion on most things, regardless.

defiance of sitting

petrol spillage energetic as lost numbers as if
    to emphasise the colour you painted home – we do something
together & the road-worn thumb through racks of convenience

two men in wheel-chairs seriously stalk a public park with
slides rollicking down the rain & spurning dreams
    a mum, for now scrunching on gravel, is hotter in trackpants
because some vibrant heaven might glow
        just out of sight, down that storm water drain

the dash dot dash in the arrangement of noise

maybe, your walk (that glade of opportunity with
spelt fictions leaping into a glimpse of
    curvature, stocking, breeze) happens regardless

& all the burnished stuff jangling in my pocket
just music to our best intentions (like you like)

i marinate a casual greeting in venom, observing your eyes
    there are no opposites

a commemorative object remains still, & again later
draws the gaze & thumps with tense inertia:
    obscene in the lovely of a weather-day suburb

we're a matinee ticket left on the chest of drawers for safe
    keeping, a jest for sure, almost laundry-liquid-concentrate

uncertainly, clouds part, showing off slicks & the stupidness of jump-rope
i had to point it out again   like the docket combo it's   good value

Z

tanya & the shell grotto

the tourist travel is always easy the ruptures the
norm, fade to a spike of wine-glass chat, post-being-
there, post-every-thing. & the plibersek patronymic
it gets her through loopholes of any geo-context,
anyway. we commune loud. we are biodiverse:
my shrouded origin is stained with effulgent soot
too! i loosen my grip on a hairstyle, bleat out the
oxymoronic messages of love, direct you outwards.

vault past the heart of a pat city state, filter out
the allocated grace out of this televised debate.
(oh that i were less responsible for generality.)
the children discovered their myth – believe it; forget
my wanton ignorance. here we are all conch-ciphers.
so develop a policy, a colonial vow, a photo of fairies.

cold logistics

it's not unlike shuffling through a curtained-printery,
grain-fed chooks scrabbling the grounds, nostradamus
glancing at you through a nervous portcullis across
the way,this projected endeavour. it's like the de-
compartmentalisation of ideas (that + some apt line &
wash illustrations). indelible stains mark every part
of your body & all the phone-calls are different
debt-consolidation-consortiums. they know your name.
whatever, it sounds sexy through a real girl's mouth.

comedy dvds are a solace come night: american
teen-loser-everyman the sub-genre of choice.
when the laser skips & flutters it's no problem,
meaning only a quick run to the forge out back.
a hearty clamour welcomes you out of the gloom
because everyone needs the environment offering
discussion with those who will act interested &
smile. abstruse conjurations afford you mental sweat
on the brow which the smithy appreciates. sparks fly
as if they were poems but really, they are not. imagine
looking tired (it's in the hair, not the eyes) on a later
makeshift couch & then uploading it as your new
profile image: antithetical to funded & lushly catered
notions of completion. it's a result, at least.

days pass like recyclable beer & pasta packaging until,
perchance, you learn reading eyes undergo a radical change
at around forty. spectacles may focus everything but
the serfs from the high-rise don't agree: three differently
themed manuscripts at the same time is your dream, &
the actualisation always will be. perhaps the economy
is just not resilient enough. your robes rustle.

a free saturday

& i'm Madonna writing a book:
framed as an honorary doctorate
(death a path through Thomas
Hardy trees this morning (glumly
boolean light; scenery jelly-data,
Eric Clapton issuing the mood:
we ought remember a certain cat,
an Irish poem, the resonances things had,
the chalky pink of bitten clinker
(but i hum vagaries in a note-to-self andante…

& the chipped mug just comes up again
like some pat Jeffery Archer twist

our senses exist for clues but all input seems
composed a season of dedications ago
(listen (one practically-a-mountain setting
is my perspective: sitting & dreaming &
sneezing in clothes (people stroll by, you know,
'i'm gonna kill this or that bastard'
(& we thought society was de-evolving

workers exude matter-of-factness angle-poised
toward fine-wines (berating what you listen to
making dreamy Marx-points to the fresh-air (well
(i love you, like Microsoft, like (shoot

we're only semi-Poe-gauche (despite
throwing a Fitzgerald party (after this

third way

your small west-of-town suburban centrist
philosophy of governance that embraces
a mix of market & interventionist philosophies
irks me every sunday. this third way you
propound (if only in thought-waves) rejects
both top-down redistribution & laissez-faire
approaches & therefore a range of bristly
academics are behind your busted imago, hiding
under the bed or something. to wit economic
governance is daft, but the stresses of technological
development feel real: education is a competitive
mechanism designed to pursue the devils (or
the capitalist-socialist hybridizers) lurking
in the details. your sexy look argues you are
in favour of neo-liberalism; the smell of chips
on the wind pursues the bottom line of adjectives
& fuzzy compromises. how i want to smile a touché.

'idioteque'

always at the end of the world strumming
the past usually self-annihilation & games
made the mind click appear more authentic
cross-referenced with something solid (kids
hid a matchbook in the long grass muddled the
syntax of time-capsules gnomes looking on
in their rendition of gnomic prognostication
(the broadway musical)) problems pop up
to a strained dance beat & i'm over 'surprise'
forthwith the lute strummer's corner of destruction
is a sweet art-deco retreat we watch documentaries
because all time is spare & plentiful strumming
at the same time denying the messages issuing
from our poor art (a regular lament the lack of
evident attack & decay in what's permissible,
what's really happening)

'in limbo'

andrew coming to this conclusion see,
fattened in some twisting sea of atonal ragas
& faces, bites his tongue: acknowledging
your twisted state (0-100 on the psychopathy
scale) marks you red with 'ineligible'. rational
& doomed to that choppy sea of decisions.

andrew bridling at the mess of his own
worth now, erotic floating atop a mosh
of darkening ears, spits: the gaudy arc
seeming to touch heaven proves a stray
nothing. we hope him happy in that
circular limbo, at least, with plenty to drink.

andrew banging out a tricksy jazz beat of
post-event reverberation (with his ears maybe),
the wily melodics indefinite, stops: often
fans stoop, think, then ask 'where should
we go now' when it ends. but they are gone,
or, simply, we can't see them (that's it).

'how to disappear completely'

take a scripted lament from
me a true desire to express
the facts about myself &
importantly that 'nothing
to express' fact. take it on
board. if i had more instructions
at hand (like a magazine like a
boy with headphones like a
million people in an airport
straggling past like the
convenience of anonymity
& grey weather) i would
misplace them. i will not
talk about my art in front
of a machine i will draw
things out i will present a
mirror as just evidence.
promises promises.

'morning bell'

with all that's gone before us (…
………) it's too easy to laugh at
all communication – the lag, that
confusion of a satellite interview,
earpieces stubbornly relaying static
(…………………………………)

my backdrop, a holiday photo-
graph stays to me a bluescreen (…
you sit at a desk…) but i can see
from this vantage in time love at
least allows the dramatisation of
a deeper schizophrenia (get away
from me…poem…i'm shuffling
this irregular time-signature out on
my drum…in a shed) being alone
might be only the most simple…

interpretation… that's enough
though, it hounds you, keeps your
hands busy (once i dreamt of a
pterodactyl that perched on my
shoulder every sunset / & now i
work out what this means (i have
the time)) that's why i admire the
overused de-climax to end things:

the fade, the placement of a more
simple image &/or sound, the
symbolic cushion or door-handle,
the bell, the (…………………)

another canberra bar / josh pyke

the sveltefringe meanders a surd sort
of alike the similitude paralysed evening
venting its clagginess: we could heart
mistletoe beneath this splurge of you:
aching unguent swift in the vomiting
left bodyspatials, support desertion
friends with frayed bandaid bladders
two looks & potentiality in singsong
elsewheresex, half & half farce
crises or dirt, mythic, pulse:
the setlist display mingling
giggles at lastly hearing ears
bland boys for saturn, we're
ex-pacifists in time, we'll
elope suck lifesavers &
swing gossamer 180s,
violin like.

waves

punch & paw out a slippery motif post
tourist hotel shots smack it down all
fourths-&-fifthsy while the event gloss
still burns white chase the midi sync
& loop up in a drizzled morning snap
to the rotodrum drone & channel it
make the pulsekickers pulse like trains
out your windowframe further outcast
yourself from the last of the generic
neighbours with several different
levels of treble & unease stew on
the ambiance & structure over coffee
generate a wash that mirrors the sun's
struggle with cloud while the mood
lasts & filter a set of harmonics to
parallel dust over the mantle bang
bliss out on the click track swing
it until dance wouldn't feel right
then effect a nightmare ocsillation
prove your point & howl:
bring about stray recognition dub
your plaintive tones high but enlist
your sister for more jaggzy lines
the hook and the breathing
don't hesitate face the sun
cresting the hedge now call
adele / jones / olaf write collage
into all cities the collaborative
dew collects a triple threat of
rave stagnation bleeding into
the annals listen softly

the lemonheads 97

evan dando wears a red rain coat
the door he hunches through chipped
& red too – any other night of clarity
you might feel walked over instead
stand soaking up a half-filled bar
a handful of students & quiet
schooners warding off a nervous edge just
cut from not eating / crowd-buzz aloneness
around these the times of going out moshpit
loose & relaxed though it befits: mellow
when stretched alterna-distant else

evan plays guitar as if
he wants to be wrapped up in bed
it's nice it's plaintive then solid
with pitch perfect distortion the
girl you're pressed close to hums
to the knowledge & it rains; a boy
that calls for a drum solo gets one;
a car, a button, a cloth great visuals for
the let down evident as you curl up into
a floor-dark morning: no quiet sleep while
the seventy minutes of loss loops:
a stellar rendition of 'break me'
always threatening to close

dinosaur jr 07

look at canberra uni bar the most stodgy
architect's midday-movie. perceive innumerable oblong ducts,
smirking through their bit-parts. goose-bump concrete
amplifies monumental presences:

2000 watts of guitar riff & said little monsters
of pre / post / oft grunge. did we mention a guitar riff?
 it's always dark we are always virtual warheads
driving the hours of lines of road to see a band
(no pressure for poetic experiences & times, but
we get tense… reason inverts).
modernity amounts to a sad commentary
on how fat, how tired, how tie-dyed j mascis looks
– singing of rabbits in response – because

we are visual reporters all of us. people touch our backs
meaning *move*, people want to see
the next guitar-riff but the result is a logical canberra pre-frost
settling atop buildings & green-space. time knits.

why write about the inaudible we wonder
(we put it to you only tightly glimpsed through this poem-space)
& *all's left to do is drink* & we do & in cubicle 2
there's poetry ranting on the door: a mass of frustrated
drives it concludes nicely being
'just really tired of pokemon'. beautiful in here,
pissing to a muted guitar riff. we urge you to plan a trip.

seriously good

our terms of engagement have altered & now
you're that beatles song but all slowed down
& done by Joe Cocker, with saxophone
& syrupy bass floating from a cathedral

oh sure, i'm taking on a studio polish too i admit
& there is no bootleg gravel cushioning our arses
no raw glass: edge of the overpass goodtimes

but at least i'm no obscure & unknown artist
& so now it's all no problem or can be;
built into a well-crafted electronica riff
we will gyrate in rehearsed frenzy, sparkling,

as being easy-listening festive attains cool

poem with no wireless networks

default kids hypnologic & semi-conic abreast the
council tree: green shirt cardboard kneed bestial

fronting the 'whatever' gregarious sun, or the limited fitting
& turning in an ex-friends outlook, quiet as synthesis

dialogue sprouts aspic coating in this turf-war muck   lisped outta
your haystack scorched koalas are insignias & form speed zones

enforce mainline agreement to wend miracles in dust
watch a band shimmy every afternoon flagrant & a half

tired   a spinning bike wheel you'd affix magnetic coils
the power of suggestion 'lipstick king' to too many boys

scared of facial analogies   a pie with sauce   red & green frogs
we leave the planet doing the same this a different that mirroring

the faux-nonchalant magazine page thongs flipped out
speed waves the dog grr   what more to return from

flickeration

walking goes long (walking through dusk
chains falling about the wayside (this hollywood
afternoon (but with a pirouette & stolen shadow
the maybes wait (you can stand & not fidget

rules vanish with breathing (with the clear night
& your accent is a separate person (looks betray
the calm sociopath as you speak (making order
out of this supposed line that flickers (& goes

bump (in the morning we are friends this making
you cry (joy or post-fucking bliss it is (the fear
of witches of mazes of (violent change being the
only way small elements are observable (for now

most of us go home (with only a few cares & patches
seeing the universe unlike it is (prevailing because

roaming capability

the mobilised youth experiment with gender talk
faster in the wake of tv retrospectives: your life
a drag though apt for tags & keyword-analysis,
while primed & drunk & environmentally ready
we sit still. anyway. et cetera. yes victor,
i'm aware amidst this jarring shift of 'voices'.
politicians are preferable &, um, things are
important. stuff is fun too like capsules of
strawberries & cream so picture past times
when intentions moved in a slightly curving
arrow (red & power-pointing straight
to the imaginary soul?)

okay, i resolve not to source lines from lateline.
no more. enough is enough. now kiss me.

i don't care don't i care care i don't. & that's a
strict observation, letting itself be seen naked,
as if by chance, to a passing group of young &
cute theories, out for a grossly-exaggerated
night on the town. what will i tell my pet john
ashbery (perched atop a shoulder) that whispers
psalms like some loony-tune devil? ply him with
stray metaphors: senators resemble helicopters,
in ways to numerous to prove? or consider
motel-soap? perhaps. the loosest underwear
ought to suffice, assist the paradox…

now being the time to admit our minor
indiscretions, to snap party-hat elastic.

the alikeness quotient

his submersion in self-harm, urban drawl & the business pages
proved only meddlesome, some might say boring.

all justified passages begin to pass as pluralised
jokes 'on you' or your co-dependants,

plaid couches instead of shady emotions looming over the coffee-
table, sprung like abstract art; the mountains of numerals

a nursery white-on-white: surely hope also is a huffing oboe?
once i implied his nickname typified 'stupor', else i might have.

we could only rescue one gram from a stray tobacco pouch
regardless & there's always more at stake, other colours. 'you can use this'

comes a voice, issuing from a wall distant as the unconscious: (& so
'found philosophy' replaces romance: figures large for a few days).

later the car won't start cresting the figurehead
of an intersection & you fall to contact with

people, hard-jaw-lines & metallic paint.
the lustre of ethereal grey h-hmmed like never before,

operatic sunlight falling flat over the shoulder
you wallow, stupid, king of car-horns.

anyone's guess is he goes about his business – me,
i'm all 'speculation with protein-bar'.

yet weird shit still trumpets out. fonts are etched into the hand.
you contract a counsellor to scoff at the advice, but secretly ponder.

even sabrina the teenage witch & skippy are ducking out
to become other tales. do you have to smoke at kid's parties?

friends abort the life/game scenario. we lose track
of themes: thistles blowsy on an aria of wind.

but everything is still there to do. eg. i waffle on, lollypop in hand,
in an improvised cellar: 'no-one orders headstones for goldfish...'

whereabouts

the horde of kids circled the cul-de-sac endlessly
on bikes, roller skates, anything with wheels, but
on the afternoon of sudden departure (when all things
were sudden in our minds) they attempted a shower of
bric-a-brac. tiny plastic figurines & comic books
were the first expressions of a devotion based on locale,
moulding so shadowed as to now appear a generic
yellow & orange blob – nothing as concrete as a smurf,
or a superman in flight.

but then the gifting became the game
& obscene objects were held up zealously.
a guiness world book of records, circa 1983,
one signal things had got out of hand; the bmx
ludicrous for it's dimensions (a removal truck
so obviously cramming itself within metres).

the final moment of farce was the nameless boy
holding a pair of underpants up from his window. but
living in a circle like that, wheeling perpetual tight curves,
it gave credence to this 'not saying things as they are meant'.
feeling is always implied & laughed off.

like paling fences built to disregard your best adulthood advance.
like a giant peppercorn that stubbornly ignores your posting,
your departure. everything is offered but nothing taken.

except the desperate expression circling

the eyes of the boy, of the underpants.

Learning about explorers

Wiradjuri in a disembodied tyre. Water is pitch. Cattle fly by in stasis. A castle of turf. Bridges from the underneath illuminate resinous purple nature. Trains are tubes of rattle. Kids shout out truants. Like deepness and darkness the curious slant of a sun. Arms are paddles. Feet are ornaments. Bends and twists eat everything alive. Slow pools & bees hide eddies malevolent. Snags often landmines put there to ward. The discretion of one icy river. No time by the wrist. Cars caught soundless. Engineers are the new lawnmowers. One pebbled beach after stones & mud. The shallows of hopeless fishers. Magpies. Starlings. Wagtails. But the sewerage sightseeing tract. Putrid green of nature. From one mini-suburb out into a thousand years. Immense brown of small scale.

Plain as hell this iceless bending in two. Liquid the same as sex. As quiet as fishing finding the major assonance here. In sand that doesn't exist. In time you don't have. The packed peaches spiking vertebrae. A passing semi & images like sex sell carbonated liquid. This point this life in time and endless impediment. Repetition floating. The first word is the first slip into the sky. A beach that never existed looms. & still perhaps doesn't appear. But something less than usual. Rural façade propped over a twisting subsistence. Sex selling salt to the people. Brewing alcohol. Keeping a horse against the odds. Meet down here and guitars ring. The singing of mint-tones to the afternoon. Drainage like sun makes a place. Never easily surrendered. A clear spot amongst controlled weeds. Wiradjuri in a disembodied tyre.

lollyology

your nails scraped down the chalkboard: a bull's eye

Scottish sheep, wrong footed by the cold, waiting for a bus,

cobbers or mates   the essence in the applicable melting point

i'm freshly showered when i leave you, fronting drizzle on the wind,

unshiverable, briefly, as physics exists to irritate us / this time of year,

here again it's vehemence, the word

a white waxed paper bag crumples – dollars

are worth more as yesteryear

approaches

random violence

burning plurals of ambulance streak through
banana roundabouts for symmetry my sedan shed-safe
the musts flowing into bubble-gum of living (just for
me) i plonk in it to dream of your more exciting memories
lines putting it in binocular focus imagining us for us
scratchy & imagistic like all the concreted places a car
could represent if the engine wasn't fucked the manifold
singular & caulk-laden   four sided squares directs vision
ever onward to cracks in the surface here's my phillips'
head appendage my opening in the back down near the
lumbar region all user-friendly & strictly signposted
exactly like a best-selling a-historical period piece & definitely
nothing else (although maybe like a pornographic magazine
my friend found once out in the bush (what was he doing there
(questions hover) the sex was weird) but he was able to fix stuff
like you & odd-jobness ipso facto seemingly a thing you must
master (not love) before moving on (to that) & this being
me never wanting to finish things like of old, a declimax,
a small moment, a clench &   depressing shudder

www.ingramcontent.com/pod-product-compliance
Ingram Content Group UK Ltd.
Pitfield, Milton Keynes, MK11 3LW, UK
UKHW020235250726
13967UKWH00001B/383

9 781105 762284